A souvenir guide

Bernard Shaw at Shaw's Corner

Hertfordshire

🍂 **National Trust**

'An eligible residence'

by Michael Holroyd

'We are in the agonies of house hunting,' Shaw wrote to H.G. Wells in April 1904. 'Now is the time to produce an eligible residence if you have one handy.' Two years later he and his wife Charlotte came across the rectory in the Hertfordshire village of Ayot St Lawrence and decided to rent it. They moved here on 3 November 1906, not believing they would stay long. But they were still here at the beginning of the First World War and eventually bought the freehold in 1920.

Below Shaw's Corner from the garden

A shy and private man

The Shaws had a large flat in London, but Charlotte insisted that her husband, who had been ill, needed plenty of country air. Shaw himself liked Ayot St Lawrence for another reason. Here was a quiet village with one shop and no bus or train station. It was also without a delivery of newspapers. This suited Shaw because he wanted to hide away from people and avoid interruptions to his work. This seemed a Shavian paradox: the famous radical playwright who attracted world-wide publicity appeared to the villagers a shy and private man. He did much of his work at the end of the garden in a revolving hut furnished like a monk's cell with a desk, chair and bunk. He could turn it round to follow the sun. Since it was a minute away from the house, Charlotte could truthfully tell callers he was 'out'.

It was difficult for the villagers to understand what sort of man he was – he seemed better known to their children and animals. But after the Hertfordshire Blizzard of 1915 he won their hearts by working hard with the other men, sawing up fallen trees and making the village tidy again. After this, they began calling the rectory 'Shaw's Corner', and later he arranged for the local blacksmith to work these words into a wrought-iron gate through which he was photographed: 'a prisoner in his own house', his housekeeper said.

One of his most charming plays, *Village Wooing*, was inspired by the village – in particular by Mrs Lyth, a widow who managed the post office. He ordered all his stamps from her with hand-written letters which she could later sell as a pension. The villagers became proud of his eccentricities – especially the dangerous manoeuvres he made on bicycles, motor-bikes and cars. He was well-guarded by his staff and did his best to conceal his financial generosity.

On 12 September 1943 Charlotte died. Shaw tried to conceal his grief but appeared extraordinarily 'caved in', the bookseller at

Ayot noticed. 'He looked very sad.' Three weeks later, when making a new Will, he offered the freehold of this ten-room house to the National Trust, and the Trust's historic buildings secretary James Lees-Milne came down to discuss this with him. The dark red-brick Edwardian rectory was no architectural masterpiece, he observed, but Shaw looked 'the very picture of the sage'.

He died on 2 November 1950 at the age of 94, having lived at Ayot for more than 40 years. His ashes were mingled with Charlotte's and scattered in the garden.

Above Shaw sawing logs in the garden

Below 'A prisoner in his own house.' Shaw at the gates of Shaw's Corner

'The harder I work the more I live'

Internationally famous and financially secure, Shaw was 50 years old when he moved to Ayot St Lawrence in 1906. A celebrated playwright, a hugely prolific writer, he was engrossed in Fabian politics and threw his energy into his work.

Intent upon making the world a better place and creating a fair society, he was appalled by poverty, inequality and the inhumane conditions in which the poor existed. He understood inequality as a direct consequence of capitalism, arguing that society was organised to enable a privileged few to accumulate vast wealth at the expense of the impoverishment of the majority. His plays use wit and irony to expose hypocrisy, ridicule injustice and highlight inequality. To ensure that his message reached a global audience, he cultivated skills in publicity and self-promotion. He became very famous, much admired and in great demand as a commentator on all manner of important contemporary issues. As well as the world of theatre, Shaw mixed with artists, politicians and aristocrats; he spoke to groups of workers and organised with others of the intellectual elite, striving to bring about socialism.

The pale Irishman

Bernard Shaw was tall, slim, with red hair, a straggly beard, pale skin and merry blue eyes. He had a melodious voice and a hearty laugh. He kept his Irish accent, and was soft spoken, polite and set great store by manners and etiquette. He was known as a very kind, generous and gentle man.

Shaw was concerned to keep himself fit and his physique in good shape. Actress Lillah McCarthy told how he 'would run around the garden doing his breathing exercises'. He cycled and used an exercise bike. He had a great passion for swimming, and when in London he swam every day at the RAC club. He found the sea irresistible, and when swimming in it, Lillah said, 'he becomes for once tranquil'.

Charlotte Shaw loved travel and they went all over the world. She hoped this would encourage her husband to rest, but Shaw would write anywhere. *St Joan* was finished on the train between King's Cross and Hatfield, and *You Never Can Tell* written from a chair in Regent's Park. On boats he would ask one admirer to fend off the others so he could write uninterrupted on deck.

Shaw used his fame and wealth not just to bring about change but also to support emerging artists, writers and musicians. Shaw's patronage supported Roger Fry to set up the Omega workshops. A tray designed by Vanessa Bell was recently unearthed at Shaw's Corner. A book for Shaw's 70th birthday pays homage from many eminent Germans including Einstein, Gropius, Mann and Zweig. Shaw was revered by millions of people, not just for his plays, but because they felt he was on their side.

A brightly burning torch

'I want to be thoroughly used up when I die for the harder I work the more I live. Life is no brief candle for me. It is a sort of splendid torch which I have got hold of for the moment, and I want to make it burn as brightly as possible before handing it on to future generations.'

GBS

Above 'There's the portrait of my great reputation,' Shaw said with a chuckle. He was painted by Augustus John three times in 1915. John considered this version, which hangs in the Dining Room, the best

Opposite Shaw in old age

Growing up in Ireland

'I saw it and smelt it and loathed it.'
GBS on the Dublin slums

George Bernard Shaw was born on 26 July 1856 at 33 Synge Street, Dublin, to George Carr Shaw and Lucinda Elizabeth (Bessie) Shaw. His sisters Lucy and Elinor Agnes were then aged three and two.

Shaw described his family as 'Shabby-Genteel, the Poor Relations, the Gentlemen who are No Gentlemen', because, although descended from eminent families, they were not wealthy. They retained the attitudes, aspirations and manners of the Irish upper class, but not the money. Shaw's father was unsuccessful in business, exacerbated by his weakness for alcohol. Shaw describes the incident which ended his childish faith in his father as perfect and omniscient:

When my father, taking me for a walk, pretended in play to throw me in the canal, he very nearly did it. When we got home I said to my mother as an awful and hardly credible discovery 'Mamma: I think Pappa is drunk' this was too much for her. She replied 'when is he anything else?'

Shaw disliked his father's name, preferring to be known as 'Bernard'.

Discovering poverty

Bessie seemed not to concern herself with her children's upbringing. 'It was a privilege to be taken for a walk or a visit with her', Shaw wrote. He was looked after by servants. One nurse took him to visit her friends in the Dublin slums. Shaw said these early visits to the city's squalid tenements laid the foundations of his lifelong hatred of poverty.

A musical family

Shaw's love of music began early. They were a musical family, and Bessie had a beautiful mezzo soprano voice, which Shaw described as 'of extraordinary purity of tone'. To learn to sing, Bessie went to George Vandeleur Lee. Lee was, Shaw said, 'a man of mesmeric vitality and force' and a 'magnetic conductor'. Having studied the physiology of the voice in his quest to understand *bel canto*, Lee developed his 'method' of voice training. He was an inspirational teacher and the combination of his skills with Bessie's beautiful voice was to prove mutually beneficial. Soon Lee was living with the Shaws, first in Synge Street and then in Torca Cottage, Dalkey. Shaw was thrilled to move to Dalkey, writing, 'I still remember the moment my mother told me we were going to live there as one of the happiest in my life.'

Above Shaw's birthplace: 33 Synge Street, Dublin

Opposite Shaw at the piano about 1876 with Robert Moore Fishbourne

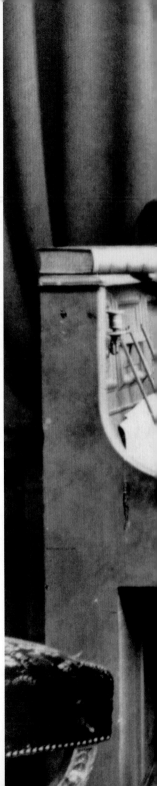

Educating himself

Shaw maintained that school taught him nothing. He couldn't remember being unable to read. School was a 'damnable boy prison'. He wrote, 'I was incorrigibly idle & worthless as a school boy & and I am proud of the fact.' He was busy educating himself, reading every book he could get hold of and learning to recognise Old Masters in the Irish National Gallery. He went to several schools and in Dublin Commercial School he met Matthew Edward McNulty, his close friend and confidant, with whom he would share his dreams of becoming an artist or a musician and discuss literature and art. By the time he was fifteen, Shaw recalled:

I could sing and whistle from end to end leading works by Handel, Haydn, Mozart, Beethoven, Rossini, Bellini, Donizetti and Verdi. I was saturated with English Literature, from Shakespeare and Bunyan to Byron and Dickens.

In 1871 Shaw started work as a clerk for Uniacke Townshend & Co. Although very capable and quickly promoted, he found the work tedious and disliked the middle-class snobbery of the office. He referred to it in his play *Misalliance*, writing, 'Of all the damnable waste of human life that ever was invented, clerking is the very worst.'

Below The view from Torca Cottage on Dalkey Hill near Dublin, where he became 'a prince in a world of my own imagination'

Early years in London

McNulty described Bessie as 'the leading amateur singer of Dublin and her house the popular resort of musicians'. But in 1873 Bessie moved to London with Vandeleur Lee, taking Agnes, then Lucy, and leaving Shaw and his father living in lodgings. Shaw sorely missed being surrounded by music and so taught himself to play the piano.

In 1876, aged twenty, Shaw followed his mother to London, arriving just days after his sister Aggy died of tuberculosis. On his arrival in London, Lucy, now a singer, helped him improve his singing and piano-playing. He went to the theatre and was invited to social events by people who came to his mother's singing lessons. Finding himself shy and socially awkward, he researched etiquette. Determined to educate himself, he frequented the National Gallery and the British Museum Reading Room.

Below Shaw's admission ticket for the Reading Room of the British Museum

Left May Morris, Henry Halliday Sparling, Emery Walker and Shaw

Opposite *The Platform Spellbinder*. Painted by Bertha Newcombe in 1892, when she was briefly in love with Shaw. Beatrice Webb described it as 'a powerful picture, in which the love of the woman had given genius to the artist'

The 'Platform Spellbinder'

This was a period of great enquiry and London thronged with new societies, clubs and lectures as long-held beliefs were challenged, and all aspects of life, society and philosophy, previously taken for granted, were subjected to scrutiny. Shaw joined the Zetetical Society in 1880, realised that he wanted to become adept at public speaking, and undertook painstaking research on his chosen topics. He would speak to any group interested in hearing him, never charging a fee and usually covering his own expenses. He was soon to become a powerful and captivating speaker known as 'The Platform Spellbinder'.

Kindred spirits

Shaw met Sidney Webb, who was to become a lifelong friend and colleague in the Fabian Society. Following Shelley, Shaw became a vegetarian. Hearing Henry George speak on Land Nationalisation, he was prompted to read Marx. In the urgent quest for solutions, the intellectual elite developed socialism as their ideology and method to achieve equality and end poverty.

Between 1879 and 1883 Shaw wrote five initially unsuccessful novels. The last, *An Unsocial Socialist*, was serialised from March 1884 in *Today – Monthly Magazine of Scientific Socialism*. Shaw wrote, 'William Morris spotted it and made my acquaintance on account of it. That took me into print and started me.' Ruskin and Morris were Shaw's heroes in art. Kelmscott House in Hammersmith was the London home of William Morris, where the Socialist League held lectures and meetings. Here was a creative atmosphere, in which art and politics were an inseparable mix, and where Shaw was to meet several kindred spirits, two of whom would become lifelong friends: Emery Walker, printmaker and photographer, whose daughter Dolly would care for the Shaws in their old age; and Sydney Cockerell, Morris's secretary, who was to become the director of the Fitzwilliam Museum and who would organise Shaw's funeral more than 65 years later. Shaw was welcomed into the Morris family circle and became a regular visitor and speaker at the Socialist League lectures. Morris's friend Andreas Scheu was to influence Shaw to take up Dr Gustave Jaeger's Sanitary System: woollen clothes as the foundation of good health.

Success

Shaw's first new clothes for years were bought with life insurance money from his father's death in 1885. 'Up until this time I was too shabby for any woman to tolerate me', Shaw said. But in his new Jaeger outfit:

A lady immediately invited me to tea, threw her arms round me and said she adored me. I permitted her to adore, being intensely curious on the subject. Never having regarded myself an attractive man, I was surprised; but I kept up appearances successfully.

The lady was Jenny Patterson, a friend of his mother and fifteen years his senior. He maintained a secretive relationship with her for the next nine years whilst also attracting a lot of attention from other women. Shaw's biographer Stanley Weintraub writes, 'According to Beatrice Webb, nearly every "advanced" female in London "worshipped at the Shavian shrine", for his romantic Irish wit and charm won over those not captured by his dialectical skill or his ideas.'

Shaw's career as a journalist was encouraged by the writer William Archer. They met in the British Museum Reading Room, when Archer approached Shaw, interested in his appearance 'as a damaged brown paper parcel on the next seat' and his reading material: Marx in French and the orchestral score of Wagner's *Tristan and Isolde*. Like Shaw, Archer was a champion of the playwright Ibsen. They were soon close friends. In 1885 Archer was able to secure work for Shaw as a reviewer of books and a critic of art, music and theatre. 'It was easiest thing in the world to get him work, because whatever he did was brilliant,' said Archer. Readers appreciated Shaw's hilarious and irreverent reviews, which were imbued with his politics. By the end of the 1880s Max Beerbohm said that Shaw was 'the most brilliant and remarkable journalist in London'. Shaw's novel *Cashel Byron's Profession* was published in America in 1886. Robert Louis Stevenson read it and wrote to Archer, 'I say Archer, my God, what women!'

As a theatre critic, his head full of Wagner and Ibsen, Shaw called for new drama to address contemporary issues, reflecting the Zeitgeist. Finding none, he set out to write it himself. In 1892 he finished his first play *Widowers' Houses*. Originally titled *Rhinegold*, the play opens on a holiday on the Rhine. Harry Trench has met and proposed to Blanche Sartorius, but her wealthy father will sanction and fund the union only if Harry's aristocratic family will accept her as an equal. Harry is appalled to learn that Sartorius makes his

money as a slum landlord and on principle finds he cannot accept such funds. As Blanche refuses to live on his 'paltry' income of £700 a year, Trench withdraws, only to become more horrified when he learns that his own income is derived from the same source.

In 1893 in his second play, *The Philanderer*, Shaw re-enacted an episode from real life, when Jenny Patterson, enraged by jealousy, barged in on his intimate romantic interlude with the actress Florence Farr. The same year he wrote *Mrs Warren's Profession*, in which Vivie discovers that her expensive Cambridge education is being paid for by her mother's chain of brothels. Shaw's plays confront the ethical dilemmas thrown up by the clash of contradicting ideology and real life. Irony, wit and sparkling dialogue are heaped upon uncomfortable truths. Amidst the uproarious laughter might linger a sense of unease as the awkward situations exposed on the stage are often those with which we as individuals and as a society have to wrestle.

Charlotte Payne-Townshend

Right Pastel of Charlotte painted in 1895. 'She is just like the portrait Sartorio made in Italy when she was in her first youth'

Below Charlotte with her cat in the 1910s

A rebel

The success in America of his play *The Devil's Disciple* brought in enough money, in 1898, for Shaw to feel able to accept the offer of marriage from Charlotte Payne-Townshend that he had rejected the previous year. Shaw and Charlotte had met in 1896, when she became involved in the Fabian Society.

Charlotte donated £1000 to the Fabian Society's newly formed London School of Economics and she agreed to lease 10 Adelphi Terrace, taking the upstairs floors to enable a school to operate below.

Common backgrounds

Charlotte and Shaw had much in common: just six months younger, she'd had, she said, 'a perfectly hellish childhood and youth' and she was an Irish Protestant. 'She being also Irish,' wrote Shaw, 'does not succumb to my arts as the unsuspecting and literal English woman does'. Unlike Shaw, however, her family was very wealthy. Charlotte blamed the death of her dear father on her domineering mother, whose outstanding ambition was to see her two daughters favourably married. Charlotte enjoyed thwarting her mother's designs and turned down several offers of marriage from prosperous suitors. Charlotte was 34, when her mother died and she gained her inheritance and her independence. She developed a lifelong love of travel and toured widely in India, Egypt and Italy, arriving in London after a failed affair with the charismatic writer Dr Axel Munthe.

'She is by nature a rebel ... sweet tempered, sympathetic and genuinely anxious to increase the world's enjoyment and diminish the world's pain.'

Beatrice Webb on
Charlotte Payne-Townshend

Supporting Shaw

A proposal

From the outset of their relationship Charlotte made herself very useful to Shaw, typing his plays and acting as his secretary. Shaw's outspoken views on women's equality and marriage led her in July 1897 to feel empowered to propose to him, to which he reacted, he wrote, 'with shuddering horror and wildly asked the fare to Australia'.

Charlotte's response was to assert her independence, demonstrate that she did not need him and make herself and her support less easily available. The following spring, Shaw, run down from overwork, succumbed to a severe infection in his foot. Charlotte returned from a six-week project in Italy to find him only able to hop around his room, which was a squalid scene of half-eaten food, unfinished manuscripts and filth. Horrified, she took charge of the situation, getting the doctor, arranging an operation and renting a house in the countryside where she could nurse him back to health.

Above **The Shaws relaxing**

Getting married

This recuperation period was also their
honeymoon. Married on 1 June 1898, Shaw
drafted the 'scoop' (unsigned) for *The Star*:
'As a lady and gentleman were out driving in
Henrietta St, Covent Garden yesterday, a
heavy shower drove them to take shelter in
the office of the superintendent Registrar
there, and in the confusion of the moment he
married them.' Charlotte brought order to
Shaw's life, organising his home environment
to support his work. This was no traditional
marriage, but rather a partnership to further
their political and literary goals.

Left Charlotte at the beach
on her honeymoon

Shaw, Granville Barker and the Court Theatre

Changing the theatre

Theatre in Victorian England had largely been light entertainment, mostly romance and sentimental comedy, in which the audience wanted to see the stars of the stage. The Independent Theatre Society, followed by the Stage Society, focused instead on drama of artistic and literary merit. Subscribing members attended 'private' performances and so avoided censorship. Shaw's play *Widowers' Houses* was first performed in 1892 on these conditions. The 'New Drama' dealt intelligently with the kind of serious social issues with which the Fabian Society was concerned, and the 'New Woman' featured heavily.

Harley Granville Barker

Handsome and talented, Harley Granville Barker was 23, when Shaw saw him acting in a Stage Society performance of Hauptmann's *Das Friedenfest* in 1900. Shaw thought 'his performance was … humanly speaking, perfect' and cast Barker to play the young poet Marchbanks in *Candida*. 'He had Shakespeare and Dickens at his finger ends,' Shaw wrote, 'He was altogether the most distinguished and incomparably the most cultivated person whom circumstances had driven into the theatre at that time.' Barker became very close to the Shaws, often visiting and taking holidays with them. Also a writer, director and producer, he developed new ways of performing Shakespeare, introducing natural speech to replace the established norm of 'ham' acting. Later he would write much celebrated prefaces to Shakespeare.

As a director, he insisted actors fully understood their characters, so presaging 'method acting'. Also an active Fabian, he saw theatre as an important contribution to society, a forum in which to raise questions and debate values and ethics, to address contemporary issues and act as a catalyst for change. To this end he campaigned for a National Theatre.

Below Harley Granville Barker about 1910

The Court Theatre, London

Between 1904 and 1907 Barker and J.E. Vedrenne
managed the Court Theatre. Vedrenne
managed the administration, and Barker stage
productions. This collaboration changed the
very nature of theatre and shaped modern
drama. Barker met Gilbert Murray, whose
translations encouraged modern performances
of the ancient Greek plays. Their first season
was a substantial bill: Euripides's *Hippolytus*,
Shakespeare's *Two Gentlemen of Verona* and
Shaw's *Candida*. Plays by Galsworthy, Masefield,
Laurence Housman, Elizabeth Robins and other
progressive writers were performed, but Shaw's
plays were the mainstay. 701 of the 988
performances given were of Shaw's plays, which
he directed himself. Barker directed the rest and
took leading roles in Shaw's plays. This created
an exciting synergy that was further enhanced
by Lillah McCarthy, often the leading lady,
whom Barker married.

London audiences were soon won over by
Shaw's work, although it took the critics a while
longer. 'To those critics who are incapable of
exercising their brains, and who have always
resented Mr Shaw vehemently, it is, of course,
galling to find themselves suddenly at odds with
public opinion,' wrote Max Beerbohm,
describing whole audiences, very happy indeed,
rocking with laughter at Shaw's swift wit: 'Mr
Shaw is an enormous success'. By 1904 Shaw
was considered England's leading playwright
and he was much in demand. King Edward VII
requested a royal command performance of
John Bull's Other Island and laughed so much
that he broke his chair.

Above Lillah McCarthy,
Charlotte Shaw and Harley
Granville Barker in 1906

Exploring Shaw's Corner

The gate announces that this is Shaw's Corner, and the door knocker shows Shaw as Man and Superman. Coming through the door with the beautiful stained-glass panel into the Entrance Hall, you step straight into Shaw's world.

The Entrance Hall

Music was vital to Shaw and sustained him throughout his long life. He loved to sing and play his piano. 'Played the second half of Die Meistersinger', 'sang a lot of songs by Gounod', 'pounded away at Beethovens ninth symphony' are extracts from his diary in January 1918. The Arts and Crafts Bechstein piano was designed by Walter Cave, secretary of the Art Workers' Guild. 'He went all the way through the score of Rhinegold on the piano', wrote Kathleen Scott, 'singing in a charming baritone voice. He plays amazingly well.'

First Night in the Stalls by Dame Laura Knight recalls the theatre audiences Shaw sought to entertain and enlighten. Shaw spent time with Laura Knight at the Malvern Festival, which started in 1929 with *The Apple Cart*, and where Shaw's plays were a major feature.

Right Shaw as 'Man and Superman'. The front door knocker was presented to him by his friend Rosie Banks Danecourt

Hats and sticks

Shaw's hats hang on the stand inside the door. His driving hat dates from his earliest motoring days. Shaw bought his first car, a Lorraine-Dietrich, in 1908, and was a keen, if erratic, driver. His bee-keeping hat was fashioned from the housekeeper's cast-offs; Shaw wore the miner's hat when he was chopping wood in the garden, a favourite pastime to keep fit. His gloves and gaiters are nearby, as are his walking sticks. One is reputedly a gift from William Morris. Morris translated the Icelandic sagas, some of Western Europe's earliest literature, esteemed by many, including Shaw and Wagner. The stick has a beautiful polished stone and an inscription from the sagas, which was an important motto for Morris and Shaw, which Morris translates as: 'Waneth wealth and fadeth friend, And we ourselves shall die, But fair fame dieth nevermore, if well ye come thereby.' Both men wanted to make improvements in the world that would last way beyond their own lifetimes.

The Arts and Crafts influence in the house, built in 1902, is immediately apparent in the Entrance Hall. Behind the door is a William Morris portière in the 'Peacock and Dragon' pattern. At the windows hangs the modern version of Morris & Co.'s 'Large Stem'. Morris curtains hung throughout the house. The hearts cut into the staircase ballusters are in the style of the designer Voysey.

Opposite Shaw's Bechstein piano and a diverse assortment of his hats

Egyptian inspiration

On the mantelpiece is an Egyptian bust, referencing some of the earliest sculpture and also the Egyptian theme of Shaw's play *Caesar and Cleopatra*.

There are several Japanese prints of birds framed asymmetrically. Shaw felt that in birds the Life Force had reached the pinnacle of beauty. Other pictures include *A Diving Swan* by Nettleship, a view of Capri and a Dürer print, *Man of Sorrows. Irish Landscape* by George Russell hangs above the Dining Room door. An enlarged set of woodcuts of birds by Thomas Bewick is displayed on the stairs.

Above Vivien Leigh starred in the 1945 film version of Shaw's play *Caesar and Cleopatra*

The Drawing Room

The south-facing windows were fitted with Vitaglass, a new material that was considered therapeutic, as it allowed in ultraviolet radiation, which ordinary glass blocked out. He also had Vitaglass fitted in his writing hut (see p.32) and in the village school.

Pictures

A portrait of Charlotte by G.A. Sartorio hangs over the mantelpiece. There are several Italian landscapes by the same artist, a Dürer print of a hare and a portrait drawing of Lawrence of Arabia, who was a frequent visitor to Shaw's Corner. Lawrence was very close to Charlotte: they sustained an intimate correspondence over a number of years. There is a small picture which Shaw labelled 'The Platform Spellbinder by Bertha Newcombe. Spellbound.'

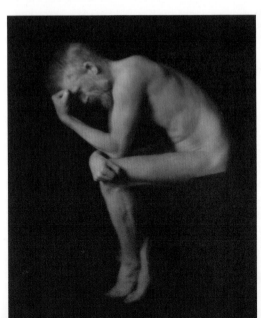

Sculpture

In this room are several sculptures, notably the bust of Shaw by Rodin. In the summer before moving to Ayot St Lawrence Shaw sat for Rodin at Meudon near Paris. Here they met Rodin's secretary, the poet Rainer Maria Rilke, and they took with them their friend, the photographer Alvin Langdon Coburn. Whilst they were there, Rodin's *Thinker* was unveiled to massive crowds in Paris. Shaw had Coburn photograph him naked in the *Thinker*'s pose. Rodin also made two line drawings of Charlotte. Rodin's bronze

Above Shaw in the Drawing Room

Left Shaw poses nude as Rodin's *The Thinker* for the photographer Alvin Langdon Coburn

of Shaw sits near his head of the writer Balzac, whom Shaw revered. His friend Packenham Beatty referred to Shaw as 'Bernardo O'Balzac'. There is also a sculpture of Rodin by Paul Troubetzkoy, who was popular amongst the theatre set. Other bronzes by him include one of a dog with a woman who is reminiscent of Charlotte, and one of Shaw. There are also small marble sculptures of Shaw's hand and a crab.

Bringing art to life

Sculpture was hugely important to Shaw, and *Pygmalion*, written in 1912, is one of his most popular plays. In classical legend, Pygmalion makes a sculpture of a beautiful woman and then falls in love with his creation. He begs the goddess Aphrodite to bring the sculpture to life, and she does so as Galatea. The Pygmalion

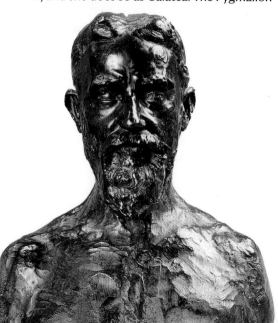

legend has been reworked many times, as a romance by Goethe, an opera by Donizetti, paintings by Goya and the Pre-Raphaelite Edward Burne-Jones, and poems by Dryden and William Morris. W.S. Gilbert staged a popular play in 1871. Shaw's version derides the class system and promotes women's rights as Professor Higgins, the phonetics expert, makes a bet that he can pass off Eliza Doolittle, a common Covent Garden flower girl, as a duchess by teaching her to speak standard English, adopt fine manners and dress up. He subverted the traditional ending to produce a strong-willed and independent woman uninterested in being the wife of her creator. He also penned the unforgettable character of Alfred Doolittle, Eliza's father, with the famous lines:

'HIGGINS. Have you no morals, man?

DOOLITTLE [unabashed] Cant afford them, Governor. Neither could you if you was as poor as me.'

Shaw won an Oscar for his screenplay of the film. He used it as a doorstop.

The Dining Room

Both the Dining Room and the Drawing Room have doors which open onto the veranda overlooking the lawn. This is a warm and sunny spot, where the Shaws would often sit with their friends. It was one of Shaw's favourite places to photograph his guests.

From the table in the Dining Room Shaw could look out over his much-loved view to the south. Lunch was said to have been a long affair, with Shaw reading his letters and deciding which ones to answer. The Shaws would always dress for dinner, whether or not they had guests. Shaw had a good collection of records, including many by his friend Edward Elgar, who dedicated the Severn Suite to him. In the evenings he would often listen to concerts on the radiogram in the corner,

telephoning the BBC to correct mistakes. Shaw himself made many radio broadcasts. There is a Morris & Co. chair, and the curtains in this room were originally 'Jasmine Trellis', a Morris design. There are ceramics by Alfred and Louise Powell. The black papier-mâché trays were gifts to Charlotte from Lawrence. A set of eighteenth-century views of Dublin by James Malton adorns the walls. The portrait of Shaw facing the window is one of three painted by Augustus John at Lady Gregory's house in Ireland. Over the serving hatch is a portrait of him by Leon De Smet.

Ornithologist and conservationist Peter Scott painted *Mallards Preening*. Scott, who founded the Worldwide Fund for Nature, visited as a child with his mother, the sculptor

Above The Dining Room mantelpiece

Right A Powell ginger jar

Kathleen Scott. Kathleen had studied sculpture with Rodin and dance with Isadora Duncan in Paris. Kathleen would teach Shaw to dance, and Shaw would read to Peter. Peter's father was Scott of the Antarctic, who died leading the 1912 South Pole expedition. Shaw's friend and neighbour, Apsley Cherry-Garrard, was a member of the same expedition who remained at base camp while Scot's small party made the attempt on the pole. Shaw helped him write his book about the expedition, *The Worst Journey in the World.* 'The Shaws taught me to write,' he said. Charlotte and Cherry shared a love of antiques and would often go on shopping trips together.

Seven photographs on the mantelpiece dominate the room. They are: Gandhi, who led India to Independence using non-violent civil disobedience; Josef Stalin, who ruled the Soviet Union from 1924 until his death in 1953 (Shaw met Stalin, when he visited Moscow in

1931); Lenin, who orchestrated the Russian revolution and became the first leader of the Soviet Union; Felix Dzerzhinsky was an early Russian revolutionary, who became the head of the Soviet secret police; Harley Granville Barker is the handsome young man who peers out at us with his arms folded. The house is 33 Synge Street, Shaw's birthplace in Dublin, and the photograph on the right is of the playwright Ibsen.

Shaw died in this room on 2 November 1950.

Above Shaw would often listen to concerts broadcast in the evening on the radiogram

The Study

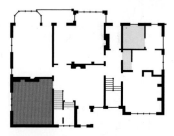

Shaw used the Study for the research that underpinned his work and for administration. His secretary sat at the smaller of the two desks.

Sidney Webb

'The ablest man in England,' Shaw said of Webb, his Fabian Society colleague. The Shaws and the Webbs visited each other annually well into their old age, continuing to work on Fabian projects. 'What a long life you and I have had, and done so much with it with the aid of our wives,' Webb wrote to Shaw in 1938. Political allies for over 50 years, Webb had been one of Shaw's political mentors. The London School of Economics, *The New Statesman* and the Labour Party all developed from Fabian ideas.

Wry juxtapositions

'[Shaw's] library reflects the extraordinary width of his interests. There is a veterinary dictionary and a political dictionary; treatises on alphabets, works on art, music, psychology, religion, travel, yoga; biographies of Chaucer, Samuel Butler, Abraham Lincoln, Napoleon, Rousseau, Saint Teresa and Wagner … The library is full of wry juxtapositions. Hitler's *Mein Kampf*, Marx's *Das Kapital*, Trotsky's *The History of the Russian Revolution*, the Bible and a polite history of the Fabian Society are no distance from one another.'

Michael Holroyd

William Morris

Morris was Shaw's other mentor, who decried Shaw's shift to the Fabians. When the Fabians' socialism failed to materialise by the 1930s, Shaw wondered if Morris had not been right after all. In the Study is a photograph of Morris by Hollyer. There is also a complete set of Morris's works, given to Shaw by May Morris, with whom he said he had a 'mystical betrothal'. May was very upset, when Shaw married Charlotte just weeks before her own divorce. The curtains are 'Kennet' by Morris & Co., the same fabric that hung in Morris's study at Kelmscott Manor, where Shaw spent Christmas in 1892.

Above left **Sidney Webb**, Shaw's friend and fellow Socialist, sitting on the veranda in 1932

Above right **William Morris**; photographed by Frederick Hollyer in 1884. Morris's daughter May described to Shaw how Morris was 'tortured' by the photographer into sitting for this portrait for the sake of the Socialist cause

Friends

A photograph shows Chesterton, Shaw, Barrie, Archer and Lord Howard de Walden as cowboys for a film made by Barrie. There are also photographs of Philip Wicksteed, whom Shaw held in high regard for formulating Fabian economic policy; Lady Gregory and W.B. Yeats, who founded the Abbey Theatre in Dublin; and the door knob from Coole Park in Ireland, Lady Gregory's home, the literary and artistic hub where Augustus John painted Shaw. Another photograph is of the Irish playwright Sean O'Casey and his family. Eileen O'Casey was one of the last people to see Shaw alive. There is also a photograph of the world heavyweight boxer Gene Tunney, whose life echoed that of Shaw's fictional hero, Cashel Byron. Shaw was always interested in boxing and became great friends with Gene Tunney and his wife, holidaying together in the Adriatic resort of Brioni.

The Aubrey Beardsley poster was commissioned by the actress Florence Farr, for her production of *Arms and the Man*. Shaw and W.B. Yeats vied for Florence Farr's affections in the early 1890s. Shaw appreciated Beardsley's art and based Dubedat, his leading character in

The Doctor's Dilemma, partly upon him. He used this play to showcase Beardsley's work and that of other artists of the Carfax Gallery: Rothenstein, John, Ricketts and Shannon.

Above **The Study**

Below Shaw wrote prolifically from the 1880s until his death in 1950

The First Floor

1 Shaw's Bedroom

Shaw's bedroom is very modest. Vandeleur Lee's 'method' recommended sleeping with a window open, and Shaw adopted this regime from his youth. When he took up the Jaeger health system, he gave up sleeping in cotton and used woollen sheets and blankets. Hanging in the wardrobe are some of Shaw's Jaeger clothes, including his famous woollen knickerbockers. His bed was designed by Ambrose Heal. At the foot of the bed hangs *Portable Altar*, a painting by the Flemish artist Leon De Smet, supported by Shaw after fleeing to Britain during the First World War.

2 The Bathroom

Shaw took a daily bath. He was meticulous about his health, weight and hygiene. Shaw was fastidious in maintaining the drains and had the water analysed regularly. He drank the German mineral water 'Apollinaris', which was his substitute for champagne.

3 The Museum Room

Originally Mrs Shaw's bedroom, this room now contains changing displays on Shaw's life and work.

War and peace: The Nobel Prize

Shaw was awarded the Nobel Prize for Literature in 1926, by which time his popularity, diminished by his attitude to the First World War, had been restored. At the outbreak of war, he had made himself unpopular by anticipating and deploring the huge waste of life on both sides, and predicting another war to follow. In *Common Sense about the War* he wrote, 'I see both nations duped, but alas! not quite unwillingly duped, by their Junkers and Militarists into wreaking on one another the wrath they should have spent in destroying Junkerism and Militarism in their own country'. Even some of his friends ostracised him. But as the war dragged on, many came round to his way of thinking.

Above left **Shaw's Bedroom**

Above **The wardrobe in Shaw's Bedroom. Shaw had strict rules about the clothes he should wear**

Below **Charles Ricketts's design for the curtain of *St Joan*, c.1923 (Fitzwilliam Museum)**

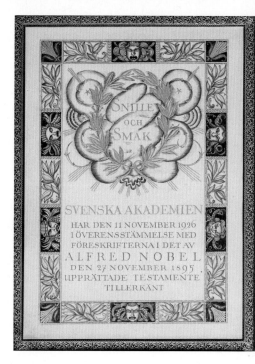
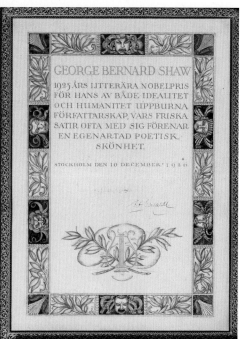

Above Shaw was awarded the Nobel Prize for Literature in 1926

Right Shaw's camera, which has recently been bequeathed to Shaw's Corner

In 1924 *St Joan* won great critical acclaim. 'It seemed to me the most wonderful first scene that I had ever heard', recalled Sybil Thorndike, who played the lead. Many consider this Shaw's finest play. The stunning set and costumes were designed by Charles Ricketts. Sheringham described it as 'one of the most beautiful things that has ever been seen on the London stage'.

Shaw was awarded the Nobel Prize 'for his work which is marked by both idealism and humanity, its stimulating satire often being infused with a singular poetic beauty'.

Photography
Shaw loved photography and owned a camera from 1895. He admired the photographs of Julia Margaret Cameron and was very close to Fred Evans. He knew and influenced Emil Hoppé and was great friends with Alvin Langdon Coburn. A prolific and devoted photographer, he wrote and lectured on the subject.

'I aspired to be a Michael Angelo and not a Shakespeare. But I could not draw well enough to satisfy myself; and the instruction I could get was worse than useless. So when dry plates and push buttons came into the market, I bought a box camera and began pushing the button.'

GBS

The Kitchen

Clara and Harry Higgs worked for the Shaws until shortly after Charlotte's death in 1943. Clara, housekeeper and cook, and Harry, gardener, were deeply attached to the Shaws and worked here until they were both in their seventies.

They had worked at Adelphi Terrace and then moved to Ayot St Lawrence with the Shaws in 1906. Shaw dedicated a book to them in 1940, writing 'To Harry and Clara Higgs, who have had a very important part in my life's work, as without them I should not have had time to write my books and plays, nor had any comfort in my daily life'. Shaw treated them with great respect: it is said that he never rang a bell to summon them but rather sought them out in person to ask for what he needed. Higgs said,

'They were like a father and mother to us.' Harry was assisted by an odd-job man, and two maids helped Mrs Higgs. A chauffeur was employed after Shaw bought his first car in 1908.

Mrs Higgs ran the kitchen, where Shaw's vegetarian meals were prepared. Shaw was a teetotaller and avoided stimulants like tea. In contrast, Charlotte enjoyed meat and fish and kept a good wine cellar. Milk, chicken and eggs were supplied by Mr Tucker at Ayot Farm next door, meat came from the butcher at Wheathampstead, and much of the fruit and vegetables were grown in the garden. Daily mealtime routine saw lunch served at 1pm, tea at 4.30pm, and dinner at 8pm. Great care went into the preparation of Shaw's food. A guest for lunch, Bertrand Russell, wrote that Shaw was served with 'such a delicious vegetarian meal that the guests all regretted their more conventional menu'.

Above The Kitchen

Left The Shaws' devoted housekeeper, Clara Higgs, with Reggie in 1941

Right Shaw pre-printed postcards with stock replies in response to the huge mailbag he received from around the world. The subjects include his vegetarian diet

Charlotte and Mrs Higgs kept very detailed records of household expenditure, which show loyal support for local suppliers and a commitment to keeping the house in good repair. The Shaws rented the house from 1906 and bought it in 1920, when they made some substantial changes. The Garden City architect Barry Parker designed and built an accumulator house to generate electricity and a garage with greenhouse attached. Shaw was a great advocate of the Garden City movement because it provided affordable, healthy homes and environments for working people. One of Ebenezer Howard's earliest supporters, he invested in them and promoted them in his plays *Major Barbara* and *John Bull's Other Island*.

The addition of the accumulator house enabled electric lights and appliances to be fitted throughout the house. This work was carried out by Bassett Lowke, whose brother owned the toy manufacturing company of the same name. W. J. Bassett Lowke produced intricate working models of trains and ships, and he was also the patron of the designer Charles Rennie Mackintosh. Mackintosh remodelled Basset Lowke's holiday cottage (called 'Candida' after Shaw's play) and also his house in Dearngate, Northampton. After spending the night in Dearngate, Shaw was asked if he had been disturbed by Mackintosh's vivid design in the bedroom. 'No', he replied, 'I always sleep with my eyes shut'.

It is impossible for Mr. Bernard Shaw to relieve individual cases of hardship. Nor can he finance elementary schools and churches. There are too many of them. His donations go to undenominational Public Bodies.

Ayot Saint Lawrence,
Welwyn, Herts.

From
Bernard Shaw
A FORTY LETTER BRITISH ALFABET

The number of letters in our Johnsonese alfabet, minus *x, c,* and *q* (unnecessary) is 23
The following consonants are missing : *sh, zh, wh, ch, th, dh,* and *ng* 7
Also missing are the vowels and dipthongs *ah, aw, oi, et, it, ot, ut, oot, yoot,* and the neutral second vowel in *colour, labour, honor, &c.* 10
40

A quite phonetic British alfabet is impossible because the vowels of British speakers differ as their finger prints do ; but the 40 sounds listed above will make them as intelligible to one another in writing as they now are in speech. Thus, though Oxford graduates and London costermongers pronounce son and sun as *san* and Ireland as *Awlnd,* they understand one another in conversation.

In Johnsonese the missing letters are indicated by using two or three letters for a single sound. For instance, *though* has six letters for two sounds. A 40 letter alfabet providing one unambiguous symbol for each sound would save manual labor at the rate of 25 per cent. per minute (131,400 per annum). Multiply this figure by the millions at every moment busy writing English somewhere in the world, and the total saving is so prodigious that the utmost cost of a change is negligible.

Children, who now have to master the multiplication and pence tables, could learn a 40 letter alfabet easily. Johnsonese is so full of inconsistencies that the few who can spell it do so not by the sound of the word but by the look of it.

Ayot Saint Lawrence,
Welwyn, Herts.

Mr. Bernard Shaw has long since been obliged by advancing years to retire from his committees and his personal activities on the platform. He therefore begs secretaries of societies to strike his name from their lists of available speakers. Mr. Shaw does not open exhibitions or bazaars, take the chair, speak at public dinners, give his name as vice-president or patron, make appeals for money on behalf of hospitals or "good causes" (however deserving), nor do any ceremonial public work. Neither can he take part in new movements nor contribute to the first numbers of new magazines. He begs his correspondents to excuse him accordingly.

Ayot Saint Lawrence,
Welwyn, Herts.

Mr. Bernard Shaw receives daily a mass of appeals from charitable institutions, religious sects and Churches, inventors, Utopian writers desirous of establishing international millennial leagues, parents unable to afford secondary education for their children : in short, everybody and every enterprise in financial straits of any sort.

All these appeals are founded on the delusion that Mr. Shaw is a multi-millionaire. The writers apparently do not know that all his income except hardly enough to meet his permanent engagements is confiscated by the Exchequer and redistributed to those with smaller taxfree incomes or applied to general purposes by which everyone benefits.

Clearly Mr. Shaw's correspondents cannot have his income both ways : in cash from himself and in services from the State. He does not complain of this, having advocated it for more than half a century, and nationalized all his landed property ; but now that it is in active and increasing operation it is useless to ask him for money : he has none to spare.

He begs to be excused accordingly. No other reply to appeals is possible.

Ayot Saint Lawrence,
Welwyn, Herts.

The Garden

Both the Shaws took their exercise in the garden. They would walk around it together in deep conversation, placing stones to record the number of laps they had made.

Shaw also enjoyed keeping fit by chopping wood. Like Shakespeare, he had a Mulberry tree and he particularly admired his Cedar and Copper Beech. Charlotte worked with the eminent horticulturalist George Jackman to design the tree planting and she planned the area at the front of the house. Charlotte liked to bring plants back home with her from her foreign travels and she sent specimens to Jackman's nursery to learn what they were and if they might thrive at Ayot.

At either end of the South Terrace are sculptures of a dog and a lamb by Troubetzkoy. In the dell is a statue of St Joan by the Shaws' neighbour Clare Winsten. The Winstens lived across the road, and after Charlotte's death Shaw would often entertain his visitors at their house. The orchard was much larger when the Shaws lived here. Apples, pears, plums and cherries were planted to give fruit from August to December. There were also walnuts and hazelnuts. What is now a car-park was then a very large vegetable patch, There was a dovecot, and, then as now, bees were kept in the garden, a section of which was left wild to encourage them. When firewood was gathered, there was

always some taken to a local widow, who had a large family to support. Bags of acorns were collected and sent to the Webbs.

Shaw took many photographs in the garden, which give great insight into his 44 years at Shaw's Corner: distinguished guests, rehearsing with Barker on the lawn, making a snowman, Charlotte asleep, positioning sculpture, choosing costumes with Gabriel Pascal for the film version of *Caesar and Cleopatra*. Shaw's photographs guide the layout and planting in the garden, which feature – then as now – delphiniums, roses and lillies.

He left a collection of over 15,000 images, which chronicle his life and which are now held at the London School of Economics.

Above The statue of St Joan in the garden

Left and opposite The garden

The writing hut

At the bottom of the garden is the revolving writing hut, which can be turned to change the view or follow the sun. This is where Shaw created many of his greatest works. He would come here every morning to write in peace and quiet.

Shaw fell in the garden in September 1950, aged 94, whilst pruning a fruit tree. In hospital for an operation on his fractured thigh, an underlying kidney disorder was discovered.

In his last days he told Nancy Astor how much he missed and dreamed of Charlotte, he spoke to Esmé Percy about Harley Granville Barker and asked Eileen O'Casey to stroke his forehead and kiss him goodbye. He died in the early hours of 2 November 1950. Shaw's last words were 'I am going to die'. Following his wishes, his ashes were mixed with those of Charlotte and scattered around the writing hut and the bottom of the garden.

This my dell and this my dwelling
Their charm so far beyond my telling,
That though in Ireland is my birthplace
This home shall be my final earthplace.
Shaw's *Rhyming Guide to Ayot St Lawrence*

Below The writing hut